UNMASKING EVIL'S HIDDEN INFILTRATION
AND EMBRACING THE POWER OF FAITH

BREAKING
the Grip of
DARKNESS

DALTON WALLEY

© 2024 Dalton Walley
BREAKING THE GRIP OF DARKNESS

All rights reserved. No part of this publication may be reproduced, stored in a retrieval system, or transmitted in any form or by any means, electronic, mechanical, photocopying, recording, or otherwise without the prior permission of the publisher or in accordance with the provisions of the Copyright, Designs and Patents Act 1988 or under the terms of any license permitting limited copying issued by the Copyright Licensing Agency.

Scripture quotations taken from the New King James Version (NKJV)®. Copyright © 1982 by Thomas Nelson. Used by permission. All rights reserved.

Library of Congress Control Number: 2024921924

ISBN: 979-8-218-51219-4

Published by:
Resurgence Publishing, LLC
P.O. Box 514
Goshen, OH 45122
www.resurgencebooks.org

Cover Design: Aaftab Sheikh

Printed in the United States of America

CONTENTS

Introduction 8

1. From The Serpent To The Cross 14

2. The Creation Of Two Nations 20

3. Esther Vs Haman: The Jewish People Delivered . . . 28

4. The Promise Of A Nation Fulfilled 36

5. Piecemeal Functionalism And A New World Order . 48

6. Choose Whom You Will Serve 62

Final Thoughts 86

About the Author 91

References 93

DEDICATION

I dedicate this book to my wife and my children. To Gwen Walley, my Wife, who is my ROCK. She is smart, wise, courageous, and beautiful. She always puts others first and is the most thoughtful person I know. I love you, Gwen.

To my hard working and big-hearted son, Devin Walley, who is held in high regard by all who know him. Devin would do just about anything for anyone in need.

To my smart and intelligent daughter, Deanna Cooke, who stays in touch with me from a good distance away but is always available when needed.

To one of the best teachers/singers in this area, my stepson James Orr, who is always ready to go above and beyond to help others.

To my very wise, smart and talented stepdaughter, Vicki Goss, a great teacher and one who is also always there to help anyone in need.

To my God, who gave His only begotten Son, Jesus Christ as a ransom for my sin so that I could obtain Salvation. All Praise and Honor is His.

MY WIFE'S REMARKS

I would like to say a few words about this book and Dalton's purpose in writing. As he stated from the beginning, he has loved and studied Bible prophecy for a very long time. God has gifted him with the knowledge and he has a goal to share and equip others with the fact that evil is real and we can't be blinded to what is going on around us! We have a voice as Christians and it is our responsibility to speak up and warn others who may not realize the dangers lurking in every facet of our lives.

We read in the new testament that we are not to be ignorant of Satan's devices and that he is as a roaring lion seeking to devour. Dalton's goal is to help educate us all to the subtle things going on around us that can catch us off guard! We are to be steadfast and unmovable in the days ahead, and recognize that even with evil infiltrating our land, God is still God and we are admonished to look up for our redemption draws nigh!

-Gwen Walley

OPENING REMARKS

This book outlines my thoughts and understanding of how Evil has always, throughout history, tried to infiltrate good. I am not, nor do I pretend to be, a writer or author of any significance. In the book, I quote a lot of material from other, more proficient writers than myself. I have tried, and hopefully succeeded, in giving credit where credit is due to the other authors I have quoted. This book is not about me or for me, and it is not written for monetary purposes. It is a simple compilation of my thoughts and beliefs, and I have pulled from several resources that I have quoted to compile a presentation in such a manner that I hope you find easy to understand and glean from.

Evil seems to be infiltrating every facet of life in today's world, and many people do not realize that it is infiltrating their lives. My hope and prayer is that some who may read this little book will come to the realization of their need for salvation through the acceptance of Jesus Christ in their lives.

INTRODUCTION

INTRODUCTION

I was nine years old when I first became interested in Bible prophecy. I grew up in church from infancy. My mother, Shellie Havens Walley, stated that she received the Holy Spirit while I was still in her womb. We attended church every Sunday, both morning and evening. I was always very attentive to what the pastor was preaching, even as a child. When I was five or six years old, I would pretend to be a preacher. In the late part of the evening after supper, my daddy, Irvin H. Walley, would say, "Baby, how about preaching us a sermon?" And me, being the ham that I was, would jump up onto the living room floor and start preaching about whatever came to mind. I would preach about the Holy Spirit, and I remember watching parishioners dance in the Spirit. Some of them seemed so happy. (We used to call this "shouting in the Spirit.")

If you were raised in a Pentecostal church during the 1950s, '60s, '70s, or '80s, you can probably relate to what I'm talking about. If not, this might be what terrified you about attending a Pentecostal service. People unfamiliar with what was happening were often frightened by these types of services. Anyway, I would preach about the Holy Spirit and how it would come down, make you happy, and cause you to shout and dance. My daddy thought my preaching was hilarious. He would encourage me with "amens," and the more he did, the more I would come up with things to preach about. Sometimes, I would retell a true Bible story I had heard from a preacher. My brother, LaBron Walley, and my sister, Carole Walley Bumpers, would ask my daddy if the stories I preached were true. Daddy would always say, "Every bit of it is true." They would reply, "I've never heard of that," and he would say, "Well, while you were sleeping in church, he was listening to what the preacher was saying."

So that gives you a little glimpse into my early life. I could tell a lot more, but I'll save that for when I write my memoirs. At around the age of nine, I realized I needed to be saved, and I accepted Christ as my Lord and Savior. That was around 1960. My pastor at the time was Reverend Norman Busby, who pastored the Bates Field Assembly of God Church in Mobile, Alabama. He and my daddy went to visit my grandfather in the hospital in Hattiesburg, Mississippi, and I had the privilege of going with them. On the way back home, Pastor Busby was telling my daddy about a place in Lucedale, Mississippi, called Palestine Gardens (which is still there today). There was a gentleman who had built a miniature version of the Holy Land, with all the cities and buildings in place, just as if you were actually in the Holy Land. The man would tell Bible stories as you walked through the miniature cities, and it almost felt like you were really there in the story. I highly recommend visiting Palestine Gardens if you're ever passing through Lucedale, Mississippi.

In 1960, Israel (the actual nation) had only been a nation for twelve years. The fact that Israel had become a nation again, as the Bible predicted, stirred many preachers of that time to become more interested in the prophecies concerning Israel's return.

Reverend Busby seemed to have a good understanding of the prophecies that were being fulfilled, and you could see them unfolding before your eyes, even in the 1960s. On many Sundays, Pastor Busby would preach about these prophecies being fulfilled.

I remember an elderly lady in our church, Sister Gaston, who was in her late 80s. She would often testify that she believed Jesus would return or the Rapture would take place in her lifetime. That stirred something in me, and I guess it scared me a little, thinking that the Rapture could happen at any moment. These were some of the things that helped propel me toward a closer walk with Jesus.

Sometime in the mid-1960s, we had an evangelist come to the Bates Field Church who was a Bible prophecy teacher and preacher. His name was A. A. Ledford, and boy, did he ever light a fire in me about learning Bible prophecy. Later, in my late teens and early twenties, I started reading about Israel and its struggles as a young nation. Every news article about Israel or the Middle East caught my attention, and

INTRODUCTION

I would compare the articles with what the Bible taught about the events happening right before my eyes. I would read anything I could find on Bible prophecy.

Hal Lindsey wrote a book titled, "The Late Great Planet Earth," which opened a lot of people's eyes to the fulfillment of Bible prophecies. Over the years, I have read many books on Bible prophecy. Some of my favorite authors include Dr. David Jeremiah, John Hagee, Jonathan Cahn, and Perry Stone, among others. I agree with most of them, though some I don't. I believe in a Pre-Tribulation Rapture, but even writers who don't hold that view still make many good points in their books. Throughout my life, I've read and studied Bible prophecy, and I would like to share with you a few of the things I've discovered in my studies.

CHAPTER 1

FROM THE SERPENT TO THE CROSS

I have discovered that from the beginning of time, Satan and his minions have tried to stop the will of God. Throughout history, evil has persistently attempted to infiltrate all of God's plans—from the very beginning to the present day. Even today, perhaps more than ever before, evil is lurking, constantly seeking any foothold it can find, even within the Church and even in your life!

What I hope to convey to anyone reading this book is a historical perspective, from the beginning of time through history up to the present day, and how evil has always tried to infiltrate God's plan. I intend to show that, even though evil has tried and has come close to destroying God's plan for the ages, we have the assurance that everything remains under God's control. I understand that not everyone will agree with what I am writing. Some have accused me of having a "doomsday mindset." However, all I aim to do is share Biblical truths, and sometimes, those truths can be painful or disturbing for some. Prophecies can be frightening, but they will come to pass as they were written. What we must remember is that, in the end, if we have accepted Christ as our Savior, we are victorious and will inherit eternal life in God's Heaven, where evil cannot infiltrate.

Let us begin with Genesis 3:1: "Now the serpent was more crafty than any other beast of the field that the Lord God had made." God had told Adam and Eve that they could eat the fruit of any tree in the Garden, except for the tree in the middle. God said, "You shall not eat of the fruit of the tree that is in the midst of the Garden, neither shall you touch it, lest you die." But the serpent (representing evil) said to the woman, "You will not surely die, for God knows that when you eat of it, your eyes will be opened, and you will be like God, knowing good and evil." The woman was deceived and believed the serpent's evil report.

What God had warned Adam and Eve about the tree in the midst of the Garden came to pass, just as He had said it would.

(This was possibly the first-ever prophecy.) As a result, sin entered the world—evil had infiltrated.

In Genesis 3:15, we read the first prophetic reference to Jesus as the "Seed of the Woman." This term is significant because all other men are referred to as the seed of Adam or the seed of man. This can only refer to the virgin birth because Jesus had no earthly father but was conceived by the Holy Spirit in Mary's womb. Therefore, Jesus is the only virgin-born human being.

Medical authorities I have read, including Louise Zabriskie in "Handbook of Obstetrics" (5th Edition, pgs. 75, 82), state the following: "The blood of the unborn child does not come from the mother but from either the father or the developing fetus itself." Since the blood of the unborn child typically comes from the father—and since Jesus had no earthly father—only Jesus can bring humanity the purity and sinlessness that Adam once had in his innocence in the Garden of Eden.

When Jesus said on the cross, "It is finished" (John 19:30), I believe He was referring not only to the completion of His earthly life but also to the fulfillment of God's plan of redemption. We all know that Jesus rose from the dead, and in doing so, evil was defeated once again.

In the following chapter, I will discuss two more examples of how evil tried to infiltrate God's plan throughout history. I will also show how evil attempted to prevent God's chosen people, the Jews, from fulfilling the destiny that God had laid out for them.

CHAPTER 2

THE CREATION OF TWO NATIONS

This chapter is drawn from "The Full Life Study Bible" (King James Version), edited by Donald C. Stamps and J. Wesley Adams, and published by Zondervan Publishing House, Grand Rapids, Michigan, U.S.A.

The editors write: "Genesis accurately records creation, the beginnings of human history, and the origin of the Hebrew people and God's covenant with them through Abraham and other Patriarchs. Its historical reliability as inspired Scripture is affirmed in the New Testament by the Lord Jesus and by the Apostles. Its historicity continues to be confirmed by modern archaeological discoveries. Moses was remarkably prepared by education and by God to write this unique first book of the Bible."

Genesis provides an essential foundation for the rest of the Pentateuch and all subsequent Biblical revelation. It preserves the only trustworthy account of the beginnings of the universe, humankind, marriage, sin, cities, languages, nations, Israel, and redemptive history. It was written with the purpose of giving God's covenant people, both in the Old and New Testaments, a foundational understanding of Himself, creation, humanity, the fall, death, judgment, covenant, and the promise of redemption through the seed of Abraham.

The covenant between God and Abraham, which began with Abraham's call, was formalized in Chapter 15 and ratified in Chapter 17. This covenant is central to all of Scripture. Genesis alone explains the origin of the twelve tribes of Israel and how the descendants of Abraham ended up in Egypt for 430 years, setting the stage for the Exodus, the central redemptive event in the Old Testament.

Genesis also reveals the prophetic history of redemption and the Redeemer, who would come through the seed of Abraham. The New Testament applies Genesis 12:3 directly to God's provision of redemption through Jesus Christ (Galatians 3:16, 29). Galatians 5 lists the descendants of Adam down to the flood, reflecting the godly line that stood for God in an increasingly corrupt age. Hebrews 11 mentions two individuals from this period—those who pleased God with their faith. These two were part of the faithful remnant who refused to go the way of Cain. By the time of the flood, nearly all hearts were evil, and only eight individuals were saved.

Moving to Genesis Chapter 11, we encounter the ancient city of Ur of the Chaldees. Located about 100 miles south of Babylon near the Euphrates River (modern-day Iraq), Ur was dedicated to Sin, the moon god (appropriately named "Sin"). In Genesis 12:3, the Bible states: "In thee shall all the families of the Earth be blessed." This is the second prophecy in Scripture concerning the coming of Jesus Christ. It speaks of a spiritual blessing that would come through a descendant of Abraham. Paul explains that this blessing refers to the Gospel of Christ offered to all nations. God's promise to Abraham shows that from the very beginning, the purpose of the Gospel was to bless all nations with salvation and goodness.

Visible appearances of the Lord are called Theophanies, or God-manifestations. The land that God promised to give Abraham was Canaan (the ancient name for Palestine), along the southeastern coast of the Mediterranean Sea. In Genesis 12:7, "And the Lord appeared unto Abram, and said, 'Unto thy seed will I give this land.' And there he built an altar unto the Lord, who appeared unto him." From this nation would come Jesus Christ, the Savior of the world, the promised seed of the woman.

God's promise and blessing to Abraham extended not only to his physical descendants (i.e., believing Jews) but also to all who, through true faith (Genesis 12:3), embrace and follow Jesus Christ, the true seed of Abraham (see Galatians 3:14-16). In other words, this includes us.

In Genesis 15:18, the Lord made a covenant with Abram. The making of this covenant is described in verses 9-17. It involved taking slaughtered animals, cutting them in half, and placing the halves opposite each other (verse 10). Typically, the two parties entering into the agreement would walk between the two halves of the animals, symbolizing that if they did not keep the covenant, they would perish like the slain animals. The smoking furnace and the burning lamp are believed to represent God's presence.

Note that while a covenant usually involved responsibilities for both parties, in this instance, only God passed between the pieces of the animal. God alone established the promises and obligations of the covenant. Abram's role was to accept them in obedient faith.

God had earlier promised Abram the land (Genesis 15), and now He renewed that promise by stating that from Abram would come many nations and kings, and that Sarai, his wife, would bear a son and become the mother of nations and kings.

Abram and his descendants were to see the fulfillment of this covenant as they bound themselves to God and the obligations of the covenant. Genesis 17:8 says, "And I will give unto thee, and to thy seed after thee, the land wherein thou art a stranger, all the land of Canaan, for an everlasting possession; and I will be their God."

Abraham and his physical descendants were promised the land of Canaan (Genesis 12:7, 13:15, 15:7, 8-21). The covenant was everlasting from God's point of view, but possession of the land was conditional on obedience to God. Later, they failed to remain obedient (Isaiah 24:5, Jeremiah 31:32), and their possession of the land was disrupted.

Genesis 25:21 records: "And Isaac entreated the Lord for his wife because she was barren, and the Lord was entreated of him, and Rebekah his wife conceived." Like Sarah, Rebekah was barren for many years, and Isaac had to pray for the next child of promise, through whom the Redeemer would eventually be born. In this way, God emphasizes the spiritual principle that redemption, spiritual inheritance, and the fulfillment of the covenant come not through natural means but through God's grace in response to prayer. Prayer, in other words, is the means by which God grants His promises and blessings.

The two nations mentioned in Genesis 25:23 represent the Israelites (Jacob's descendants) and the Edomites (Esau's descendants). Hostility characterized their relationship, as Esau's selling of his birthright revealed how little he valued God's blessings and covenant promises. He foolishly traded future, long-lasting blessings for momentary pleasures. Jacob, on the other hand, desired the spiritual blessings of the future, and from him came the twelve tribes of Israel.

CHAPTER 3

ESTHER VS HAMAN: THE JEWISH PEOPLE DELIVERED

Skipping ahead to the story of Joseph and the Israelites' bondage in Egypt, we see that later the Israelites failed to obey God's covenant. Consequently, they were scattered to Egypt and placed under bondage. In Exodus 1:7, "And the children of Israel were fruitful, and increased abundantly, and multiplied, and waxed exceedingly mighty, and the land was filled with them." But a new king arose in Egypt who did not know Joseph—one who represented evil.

The book of Exodus continues the story of God's dealings with the Israelites that began in Genesis. The time gap between Joseph's death and the beginning of Israel's persecution by the Egyptians was approximately 220 years. If we place the date of the Exodus around 1449 B.C., the Pharaoh who "knew not Joseph" was likely Thutmose I (1539-1514 B.C.). The Pharaoh of the Exodus would have been Amenhotep

II (1447-1421 B.C.). The Israelites remained in Egypt for 430 years, just as prophesied.

In Exodus 1:15, the king of Egypt spoke to the Hebrew midwives, Shiphrah and Puah, and commanded them to kill all male Hebrew babies. However, the midwives feared God and did not do as the king commanded, saving the male children. In return, God blessed them. This attempt by Pharaoh to eliminate the Israelites was yet another example of evil infiltrating to stop God's plan—but it failed, just as it had before.

As we move forward, I will show another time in history when evil attempted to stop the lineage of God's promise to the Israelites (the Jews).

THE STORY OF ESTHER AND ITS RELEVANCE

The Book of Esther presents a profound example of God's providential care over His people, even in the face of annihilation. The dramatic unfolding of events is a testament to how God works behind the scenes to protect and preserve His chosen ones, even when His name is not explicitly mentioned. Haman, a representative of evil, plots to destroy the Jews, much like the Antichrist foretold in the New Testament will seek to destroy both Jews and Christians. Yet, as history shows, God's plans always prevail.

The theme of evil infiltrating God's plan, as seen in the stories of Esther, Joseph, and Moses, has been a constant throughout the Bible. The enemy has attempted to thwart God's purposes, but has ultimately failed. This struggle is not limited to ancient times; it continues to this very day. The animosity toward the Jewish people and the efforts to destroy them are not merely a historical phenomenon. Even in the modern era, attempts to harm the Jewish nation continue.

However, just as God used Esther and Mordecai to protect the Jewish people, His sovereignty remains in place today. The story of Esther foreshadows the protection and deliverance promised to believers in Christ, who are called to stand firm in the face of persecution and adversity.

MODERN PARALLELS AND THE ONGOING STRUGGLE

As we examine the events of Esther's time, we can see clear parallels to today's world. The battle between good and evil continues, and history repeats itself in various forms. Just as Haman sought to destroy the Jewish people in Persia, so too have many leaders and nations throughout history sought to harm God's chosen people. The Holocaust, the ongoing conflict in the Middle East, and the rise of Antisemitism in recent decades are all evidence of this persistent evil.

Yet, the message of Esther provides hope. God's plans cannot be undone by the schemes of men. His covenant with Abraham and his descendants stands firm, and His promise of redemption through Jesus Christ offers hope to all who believe, Jew and Gentile alike.

LOOKING FORWARD: A CONTINUED STRUGGLE

As we move through history, it is important to recognize that the battle between good and evil is not yet over. In fact, it intensifies as we approach the end of the age. The New Testament warns of an increase in persecution and tribulation, especially for those who follow Christ. The book of Revelation, in particular, describes a time of great suffering, but it also offers the assurance that evil will ultimately be defeated.

The examples from the Old Testament—whether it is Joseph being sold into slavery, Moses facing the oppression of Pharaoh, or Esther confronting the plots of Haman—illustrate the enduring truth that God is always in control. Despite the infiltration of evil, God's plan will be accomplished, and His people will be delivered.

As we look toward the future, we can take comfort in this truth. Though evil may seem to prevail at times, God's ultimate victory is assured. Just as He preserved His people in the days of Esther, He will continue to do so until the end of time.

LOOKING CLOSER AT HISTORY: A MORE RECENT STRUGGLE

Now that we've explored the biblical examples of evil's attempts to infiltrate and destroy good, let's shift our focus to more recent history. The patterns of persecution, hatred, and the infiltration of evil that began in the Old Testament have persisted through the centuries. The atrocities committed against the Jewish people during the Holocaust, the rise of totalitarian regimes that sought to erase faith in God, and the ongoing conflicts in the Middle East are modern-day examples of this age-old struggle.

In each of these instances, we see evil trying to overcome good, much like in the stories of Moses, Joseph, and Esther. And yet, just as in those biblical narratives, God's hand of protection has been evident. Despite the overwhelming odds, the Jewish people have survived and thrived, and God's promises remain intact.

CONCLUSION: EVIL'S ONGOING FAILURE

Throughout this exploration, one thing has become abundantly clear: evil has consistently tried to infiltrate and destroy God's plan, but it has never succeeded. Whether through Pharaoh's decrees, Haman's plots, or modern-day persecution, evil has been unable to overcome the providence of God. God's plan for redemption, which began with Abraham and culminated in Jesus Christ, remains unshaken.

As we move forward, we must remember that while evil may continue to infiltrate, it will never ultimately prevail. God's promises are sure, and His people will be preserved. Our responsibility, as believers, is to remain faithful, to trust in God's sovereignty, and to stand firm in the face of adversity, knowing that the victory has already been won through Jesus Christ.

This ongoing battle between good and evil, which began in Genesis and continues through the story of Esther and beyond, serves as a reminder that we are part of a much larger narrative. It is a narrative in which good will ultimately triumph over evil, and God's kingdom will be established forever.

CHAPTER 4

THE PROMISE OF A NATION FULFILLED

To help you understand the key ideas in the remainder of this book, here is a list of definitions to ensure that the concepts we discuss are easy to follow and understand throughout the chapters ahead.

Cabal: A "cabal" refers to a small, secretive group of individuals who unite to advance their private interests, typically in politics, an ideology, or within a community. This term often carries negative connotations, suggesting conspiracy, intrigue, and manipulation that occur out of public sight. Cabals generally work covertly, promoting their agendas without the knowledge of the broader public.

Deep State: The "deep state" refers to a group of people, often within government or military institutions, believed to operate behind the scenes, manipulating or controlling governmental policies without public accountability. These individuals are perceived to influence decision-making processes in secret, outside of the democratic system.

Shadow Government: A "shadow government", sometimes called a secret or invisible government, is the idea that the real political power does not reside with publicly elected officials but instead with private individuals or entities operating behind the scenes. These entities control key decisions and actions in governance without the scrutiny or oversight that democratic institutions would normally provide.

Oligarchy: An "oligarchy" is a form of governance where political power is concentrated in the hands of a small group, usually the wealthiest, most influential, or militarily powerful individuals. These individuals exert control over decision-making processes, often at the expense of broader democratic participation, and they prioritize their interests over those of the majority.

These are some facts that I have discovered from my studies of prophetic scripture:

» Israel has a right to Her land – (Deut. 11:12)

THE PROMISE OF A NATION FULFILLED

- God defined the boundaries – (Gen. 15:18)

- Israel belongs to God – (Lev. 25:23)

- God has promised to protect and defend Israel – (Isaiah 31:5, Ps. 121:4, Zech. 12:2-9)

- God gave Israel to the Patriarchs (Abraham, Isaac, and Jacob) and their descendants – (Gen. 12:7, 17:7-8, Ps. 89:30-38, Deut. 7:7-9, Gen. 28:4, 28:13-15, 35:9-15, 36:6-9)

- Israel's captivity did not change their divine right to their land – (Deut. 30:1-5, Amos 9:14-15, Lev. 26:40-45)

- The correct and legal name of this land is not Palestine but ISRAEL – (Ez. 37:11-12)

- Jerusalem is called "The Apple of God's Eye" – (Zech. 2:4,5,8)

- Jerusalem belongs to the Jewish people – (Zech. 8:4-8)

- Messiah will come to Jerusalem – (Zech. 9:9, 14:14)

- God will destroy all Nations that come against Jerusalem – (Zech. 12:2-9)

These are words of hope, assurance, and comfort. The psalmist wrote, "Forever, O Lord, thy Word is settled in Heaven" (Psalm 119:89). So why should we worry?

Israel yields to a much higher authority than the U.N. or any other body of men, including the World Economic Forum. The words of the Lord God of Israel cannot be changed by a mere mortal. No one has the right to violate God's promises to Israel.

Israel is the main focus of watching, knowing, and understanding the times in which we live. After the destruction of Jerusalem and following the resurrection of Christ, Israel was scattered throughout the world. (This is where the Gentile dispensation or Grace dispensation began).

A.A. Ledford, in his book ("Pathways to Prophetic Fulfillment", Copyright 1978 by Pathway Press), writes about Captain Alfred Dreyfus, and I verified the story from Wikipedia. The story goes as follows:

Since 1907, the Jewish Nation has slowly returned to its Homeland. Treaty by treaty, war by war, and agreement by agreement, they have become what they are today.

Let's take a trip back through history to search and learn how the Israelite Nation, after the Diaspora (the dispersion of the Jewish Nation), was divinely brought back to their Homeland. This fulfills what was prophesied in the Bible (Matt. 24:32-45)—to become the end-time nation that would be present when Jesus returns.

THE BEGINNING OF A FLICKER OF PROPHECY

I believe divine intervention began to take shape in 1893. History tells us that a military court conducted a trial of Captain Alfred Dreyfus in 1893. Dreyfus, a French officer, was accused of selling secrets to the enemy. However, this trial was not about facts, but about his Jewish heritage. Essentially, the court was trying him because he was Jewish, even though he was innocent of the charges.

Dreyfus maintained his innocence, but he was found guilty and sentenced to life imprisonment on Devil's Island. Two years later, the soldier who was actually responsible for the crime confessed, but the French government refused to accept his confession. For unknown reasons, Dreyfus remained imprisoned until 1906.

During this trial, a journalist named Theodor Herzl from Budapest, Hungary, was assigned to cover the story in Paris. As Herzl sat through the trial, he was deeply disturbed by the injustice he witnessed. He saw that this was not merely a trial of guilt or innocence but of identity—Dreyfus was being persecuted because of his Jewish background. ("2)

Herzl returned home and, unable to shake the feeling of impending doom, began publishing a small informative paper titled Jewish State. The materials were sent to Jews worldwide, helping to stir a greater awareness of their plight.

THE BIRTH OF THE ZIONIST MOVEMENT

Herzl's efforts grew, and in 1897 he called together more than 200 delegates to a conference in Basel, Switzerland. This was a monumental moment, marking the formal birth of the Zionist Movement ("4). Herzl had ignited a fire that would eventually lead to the Jews returning to their homeland.

One of the readers of Herzl's publications was Chaim Weizmann, a prominent Jew in British circles. Weizmann played an instrumental role in advocating for the Jewish homeland. He provided a formula for TNT, derived from cornstarch, which significantly contributed to the British war effort in World War I.

THE BALFOUR DECLARATION

At the same time, a British diplomat named Arthur James Balfour was a key figure in supporting the Jewish return to their homeland. Balfour, influenced by his Anglican upbringing, had been taught that Israel must be regathered to its land before the Lord could return. This teaching had a profound impact on him.

On November 2, 1917, Balfour drafted what is now known as the Balfour Declaration, which called for the establishment of a Jewish homeland in Palestine. Parliament passed the declaration immediately. ("3) This declaration would eventually come at a great cost to the British government, involving the loss of soldiers and significant financial expenditure.

Herzl had predicted earlier that within 50 years, the Jews would significantly affect world politics. Remarkably, 50 years, nine months, and fifteen days later, Israel declared its independence. On May 14, 1948, at 4 pm, David Ben-Gurion raised the Israeli flag, and within 11 minutes, President Harry Truman recognized Israel as a nation. ("3)

The British and the Liberation of Jerusalem

After the passing of the Balfour Declaration, the British government sent General Edmund Henry Allenby to carry out the declaration's intent. On December 9, 1917, General Allenby prepared to invade Jerusalem. Mysterious events occurred that many regard as divine interventions. Turkish forces, who had held the land since 1516, suddenly abandoned the city.

One of the most notable events was the sudden appearance of British airplanes. The Turkish soldiers, having never seen planes before, were terrified. This and other unexplainable incidents—such as barrels of rocks mysteriously rolling down hills—caused the Turkish Army to surrender Jerusalem to the British without a single shot being fired. ("6)

THE RELUCTANCE OF JEWS TO RETURN HOME

Though the Balfour Declaration gave the Jewish people the right to return to their homeland, many were reluctant to leave the comfortable lives they had established in other countries. ("6)

THE RISE OF ADOLF HITLER

In 1922, a young man who had been a paperhanger by trade decided to enter politics. This man, born in Austria, made the bold proclamation that he would one day become Germany's greatest leader. His name was Adolf Hitler. Although Hitler initially failed to win public office, he was advised by his friend, Karl Lueger, to take a public speaking course to learn how to sway the masses.

Hitler took this advice, and by 1933, he was named Chancellor of Germany. In 1934, after President Paul Von Hindenburg passed away, Hitler took control of the German government. Over the next several years, he organized the Nazi Party and the Third Reich, spreading his influence across Europe.

Hitler's fanatical vision of world domination led to the horrors of the Holocaust. He sought to exterminate the Jewish people, killing over six million Jews during World War II. His actions are reminiscent of the evil described in biblical accounts of those who sought to destroy God's chosen people.

THE HOLOCAUST AND ITS AFTERMATH

The atrocities of the Holocaust reawakened the Jewish people's desire to return to their homeland. This longing to re-establish the nation of Israel had been prophesied over two thousand years ago.

In conclusion, from Genesis until the present age, evil has continually sought to infiltrate and destroy God's divine plan. History shows how time and again, evil forces like Hitler tried to eliminate God's chosen people, but they have always failed. These historical events only serve to reinforce that the prophecies of the Bible are being fulfilled.

I have intentionally skipped over many significant and fascinating parts of history to emphasize a central point: from the time of Genesis to the present day, evil has continually sought to infiltrate and disrupt God's plan. This battle between good and evil isn't limited to grand historical events; it extends down to the individual level. Evil is always lurking, not only trying to derail God's eternal plan but also seeking to harm each of us personally.

As you read these words, I sincerely hope and pray that you recognize Satan's intent to destroy us all. But there is hope. I urge you to turn to Jesus, ask for His forgiveness, and accept Him as your Lord and Savior.

CHAPTER 5

PIECEMEAL FUNCTIONALISM AND A NEW WORLD ORDER

Israel is what it is today because of the wars, negotiations, treaties, and agreements that have instilled in its people a desire to return to their homeland. This process has been ongoing since 1907. Over the years, they have slowly trickled back to the land that God promised to Abraham and his descendants.

The Israeli nation was declared on Friday, May 14, 1948. On June 7, 1967, Jerusalem was captured by the Israeli Defense Forces (IDF), and from that time on, the Jewish nation (State) was no longer under Gentile control.

The Bible tells us that when you see Israel becoming a nation again (the budding of the fig tree, as noted in Matthew 24), the Rapture is near. The term "Rapture" refers to the catching away of people who have accepted Christ as their Savior. The Bible further declares that the generation who witnesses this occurrence—Israel becoming a nation again—will not pass away before the coming of Christ, referring to the Rapture.

Let's review a bit more history to understand where we are today. When the European Union was formed, it began with an agreement on the production of coal and steel. It then evolved into the European Common Market, and today it is called the European Union (EU). This entity will likely soon elect a leader who could be referred to as the President of the Union. This development undermines the sovereignty of all the countries involved and brings about a revised Roman Empire, which the Book of Daniel describes so aptly—a concept many Christians may have been taught before.

In my studies, I have discovered and previously taught about "Piecemeal Functionalism." This theory explains how the results that the Bible discusses are being manipulated—Satanically—through a process called "Management by Crisis." The individuals in charge (not limited to Congress or the Senate) include organizations such as the Trilateral Commission, the Council on Foreign Relations, the United

Nations, the International Monetary Fund, the World Trade Organization, the World Bank, NATO (North Atlantic Treaty Organization), NAFTA (North American Free Trade Agreement, now called the United States-Mexico-Canada Agreement or USMCA), OPEC, the World Economic Forum, and groups like Skull and Bones, along with oligarchies in other countries. These entities constitute what is often referred to as the Deep State and many shadow governments that are influencing the duly elected government of the people.

These organizations create situations that people would not normally accept or support but will comply with due to a manufactured crisis, such as the economic bailout in 2008.

Since the bailout, the government has gained control over banks, some of the largest insurance companies, and many other financial institutions. Eventually, they will exert control over every segment of society, which means that you and I will be beholden to them; it is a move toward a world government.

A pertinent example is the COVID-19 pandemic of 2020. The entire world shut down, and everyone was required to obey government mandates. If you didn't follow these mandates, you were not permitted to enter stores or any public places. Churches were closed. If you didn't wear a mask or could not prove you had been vaccinated, you were barred from most buildings. This period was wholly controlled by the government.

In my opinion, we are living in a time where globalism is becoming more prevalent and accepted as a way of life. The Bible states that in the last days, there will be a one-world government led by the Antichrist.

According to biblical prophecy, that is precisely what will happen. With the rise of technology, artificial intelligence, and communication devices, the world has seemingly shrunk. Governments are increasingly compelled to cooperate due to various global crises, and nations are setting aside their nationalist rights to unite, which is pushing us toward globalism.

When the Antichrist appears, he will provide solutions to the world's financial problems and other issues. The world will be eager to accept him as a messianic figure (Revelation 16). By the way, I won't be here when he reveals himself; I will have already been taken in the Rapture.

The entities I have mentioned are collaborating to establish a world currency or economy, possibly in the form of Bitcoin or some type of digital currency. Cash may soon become obsolete, replaced by something known as Special Drawing Rights (SDRs). You can search online for more information on SDRs. It is crucial that you understand this concept; while SDRs have existed since 1969, they have yet to be used extensively on an individual basis. They fall under the authority of the International Monetary Fund.

Although these entities may not appear to be working in concert, they are united in their goals, controlled by wealthy and powerful individuals. They will likely need to collapse the economies of the world to achieve their aims. Our government is currently thirty-five trillion dollars in debt and is accumulating over a trillion dollars a year. If the Green New Deal is enacted, it could drive our debt up an additional hundred trillion dollars. At that point, if not sooner, our debt will become unsustainable, necessitating a revamping of our monetary system. Eventually, we will be compelled to adopt a world currency.

Senator John Kennedy, representing the state of Louisiana, stated on Fox News that the United States is borrowing a million dollars a minute. As mentioned earlier, the U.S. deficit is increasing by more than one trillion dollars a year. How long can this continue? Just to illustrate the enormity of a trillion: if you started spending a million dollars every single day since Jesus was born, you still wouldn't have spent a trillion dollars. Another mathematician puts it this way: one million seconds is about 11.5 days, one billion seconds is approximately 32 years, while one trillion seconds equals about 32,000 years (according to http://www.nasa.gov/WWW/K12/numbers/Math/Mathematical_Thinking/how_big_is_a_trillion.htm).

PIECEMEAL FUNCTIONALISM AND A NEW WORLD ORDER

These entities will also, for the sake of peace, create a world religion—a secular religion. Some are already labeling global warming as a religion. Many national leaders and so-called elites, including movie stars, major sports figures, media personalities, and numerous elected officials, are now turning to Kabbalah rather than the Bible. Most of you may not have heard of Kabbalah, but it is vital that you know about it. Be alert!

Finally, while these entities may seem to focus on different aspects of people's lives, they are collaborating to form a world government. This is where I will likely be accused of being a conspiracy theorist. To my accusers, I say: check the facts. In my opinion, these are evil infiltrations.

If you believe in a pre-Tribulation Rapture, you had better prepare to leave this world, as events are unfolding rapidly. By the time you read this book, some of the matters we will discuss may have already occurred.

I believe that there will soon arise a need for a world leader to guide the New

World Order. So, let's discuss what the near future holds according to the Bible.

When the Gulf War ended, President George Bush's vision for a New World Order seemed within reach. Bush envisioned a time when nations could resolve their differences without war and bloodshed, hoping for an era in which nations could work together for the common good. These were noble goals, but they faded under the harsh realities of a world recession and growing demands for nationalism and protectionism. Although there was general agreement in theory on an international community without barriers or borders, recent decades have seen wars between Croats and Serbs, Armenians and Azerbaijanis, Irish Protestants and Catholics, Sunnis and Shiites, and many other ethnic and religious groups prioritize self-preservation over international cooperation.

People wonder what it will take to bring peace to this earth. Are the problems so overwhelming that the systems we have established for peace and stability are inadequate? Can we resolve these issues?

As the world sinks into a mire of moral failure, environmental disaster, and ethnic tension, the need for a strong world leader will become increasingly evident.

History shows that many world leaders have risen to power during times of unrest. Napoleon took control of France following the failed French Revolution. The Germans rallied around Hitler as the supposed savior of their nation during the Great Depression and the humiliation following World War I. Lenin and Stalin gained control of Russia by exploiting the frustrations of oppressed masses, promising economic stability and security. Economic hardship and political instability often breed national so-called messiahs who unite their followers with promises of salvation from ruin.

The Bible describes an individual who will play a major role in God's end-time scenario for the world. This person is referred to by several names: "the ruler who will come" (Daniel 9:26-27), "the man of lawlessness" (2 Thessalonians 2:3), "the Antichrist" (1 John 2:18), and "the Beast" (Revelation 13:2). The Bible provides a detailed description of an individual who will mesmerize the world to the point of total acceptance. This diabolical figure will lead a final rebellion against God in a last-ditch effort at evil infiltration. I could elaborate on how he will come to power, but that would require another book.

Unstable times will demand strong leadership. Powerful leaders will be imperative to impose order amid the ongoing chaos. This individual will be able to compel most countries to capitulate to a unified Europe, thereby bringing about a revived Roman Empire. He will be recognized for his success in uniting Europe.

The world will view his efforts to promote peace in the Middle East and to broker a settlement between Israel and her Arab neighbors as essential to avoiding a potential powder keg.

All his actions will appear prosperous, as though God Himself were pleased with him. He will think in global terms and make strategic decisions that will cause most of the world to marvel at his power and influence.

PIECEMEAL FUNCTIONALISM AND A NEW WORLD ORDER

Over 2,000 years ago, the Apostle Paul identified him as the man of lawlessness. Today, most would call him the Antichrist. If God's end-time program is indeed near—and I strongly believe it is—the Antichrist is likely alive and in some position of power (I emphasize "likely"). His identity will not be revealed until he signs a seven-year treaty with the nation of Israel. Again, I firmly believe that the Rapture will have occurred by that time. I admit I do not know this as fact; I am stating it as my opinion. Your views may differ, but the essential point is that we must be saved, regardless of when these events unfold.

Satan is the prince of darkness, yet Paul warned in the book of Corinthians that "Satan will masquerade as an angel of light" (2 Corinthians 11:14). The undiscerning can easily be fooled by Satan's outward appearance. It is only after it is too late that they realize who he truly is. The Antichrist will be guided and gifted by Satan, who will provide cover for his evil infiltration. Again, Christians will not be present when this occurs; we will have been raptured. Very likely, the covenant mentioned in Daniel chapter 9 will allow Israel to coexist peacefully with her Arab neighbors. One outcome of this covenant is that Israel will be permitted to rebuild her Temple in Jerusalem.

Jerusalem was recently recognized as the capital of Israel, so you can see that events are coming together rapidly. This world ruler will succeed where previous leaders—such as Kissinger, Carter, Reagan, Bush, Clinton, Obama, Trump, and Biden—have failed. While the world watches for a tyrant, the Antichrist will present himself as a trusted leader who promises peace.

As we watch and read the news, we see with our own eyes and hear with our own ears the descendants of Isaac (Israel) and Ishmael (the Palestinians) signing peace agreements. Soon, "the dead in Christ shall rise first, and we who are alive and remain shall be caught up with them to meet Christ in the air." So shall we ever be with the Lord. Even so, come, Lord Jesus, is our prayer.

CHAPTER 6

CHOOSE WHOM YOU WILL SERVE

My purpose for this book is to awaken both believers and non-believers from their complacency. In my opinion, time is running out—specifically, the time before the Rapture.

Mankind faces a clear choice: you will either spend eternity in horrible torment or experience everlasting happiness and eternal life. My goal is to illustrate that evil has been present since the beginning of time and continues to be so today. I have only begun to scratch the surface of what life would be like if you were to fall for and accept the evil infiltration that is so prevalent now. Based on the best available intelligence and prophetic scriptures, I will share some of my thoughts in the pages that follow.

As I attempt to inform you about the current happenings in our world, I hope you will recognize the evil infiltrations occurring in and around our lives.

Former President Barack Obama began his rise to power by following a man named Saul Alinsky, who is often regarded as the father of community organizing and American socialism. Hillary Clinton was also a strong proponent of Alinsky's socialist beliefs; she even chose his work as the topic for her Wellesley College thesis in 1969. According to a 2007 article in the "Boston Globe", Clinton interviewed Alinsky on two separate occasions for the paper titled "There is Only the Fight." The following information provides an analysis of the Alinsky model.

Alinsky stated that he could never accept any rigid dogma or ideology, whether it be Christianity or Marxism. Below is a summary of Alinsky's rules for organizing a socialist state:

1. Control health care, and you control the people. Strive to increase the poverty level to its maximum potential. The poor are easier to control and have a much lower resistance level when their needs are provided for.

- My Thoughts: Consider ObamaCare, or the Affordable Care Act (ACA). In the insurance industry, we often refer to it as the "Unaffordable Care Act." Unless someone is impoverished and receives a government subsidy, most people cannot afford the premiums or deductibles. Now we see radical left-leaning politicians calling for "Medicare for All." While that sounds appealing, it is impractical. If Medicare for All were to succeed, it could add several trillion dollars to our national debt, which is already at 35 trillion. At some point, we will struggle to pay even the interest on this debt, ultimately leading to an economic collapse.

2. Allow debt levels to soar to unsustainable levels. This will facilitate the leverage of taxes, leading to an increase in poverty.

- My Thoughts: If the radical left's proposals for Medicare for All, free college education (which I view as indoctrination), and the Green New Deal are implemented to combat global warming and manage the influx of illegal immigrants, the associated costs will again lead to economic collapse.

3. Remove the means for the masses to rebel or defend themselves by outlawing or seizing their guns. This is a necessary first step in creating a police state and solidifying absolute control.

   – My Thoughts: Once more, radical leftist liberals are calling for gun control and the confiscation of all firearms. This push is currently being championed by the Democratic candidate for President of the United States as I write this, and it is a frightening prospect.

4. Establish the "true" welfare state by providing food, housing, and income for the majority of the people.

   – My Thoughts: As a nation, we now provide for not only our own less fortunate citizens but also for hundreds of thousands of illegal immigrants crossing our borders daily, further contributing to our growing national debt.

5. Obliterate all references to and images of God and organized religion.

   – My Thoughts: Again, the radical left seeks to remove God from our society.

They label Christians and those who uphold Christian values as "religious bigots."

6. Create and encourage class warfare between the wealthy and the very poor. The obvious goal is to generate discontent, allowing the government to tax the wealthy and redistribute resources to the poor through social programs.

- My Thoughts: Those of us who work for a living are already taxed to the maximum. We pay federal, state, county, and city taxes, along with taxes on food, clothing, vehicles, schools, land, phone services, and the internet. When you tally all these taxes, very little of your income remains for spending.

Does this sound eerily familiar to what is happening in today's world? It reads like a script from the far-left political machine. Politically speaking, we have a choice: do we want an America that remains a free capitalist society, or do we prefer a nation of socialism? So far, socialism has failed everywhere it has been tried.

Satan and his minions are attempting to create conditions for a total collapse of the world's financial infrastructure, thereby generating an urgent need for a new world currency. Mayer Amschel Rothschild, the founder of the Rothschild dynasty, is quoted as saying, "Let me issue and control a nation's money, and I care not who makes its laws." It is clear that whoever controls the money controls the country—or, in this case, the world.

In reality, the dollar, like other major currencies, is not backed by gold or silver but by the blind faith of the people. This faith is all that makes it acceptable for trade and commerce. In my opinion, all it would take to collapse the world's financial system is the widespread realization that paper money is... just paper.

The satanic cabal, working to destabilize the United States, operates through unofficial alliances that all stand to gain from America's fall. International banking entities and other global interests partner with willing accomplices in the United States. These individuals occupy powerful positions within the federal government and hold influential roles in many European governments. They are loyal to the multi-billionaires who recruited them to advance their socialist agendas—what I refer to as evil infiltrations.

These power brokers fund liberal progressive candidates and promote left-leaning policies. They spend staggering amounts of money to defeat conservative candidates and block the passage of fiscally responsible, freedom-preserving legislation. Those who share this agenda manipulate highly placed figures in government. In the United States, these partners—often referred to as the deep state—include approximately three hundred of the most powerful officials in Washington, D.C., spanning Democrats, Republicans, and Independents.

It is important to recognize that the carefully planned agenda to weaken America did not begin in 2008. This political-economic agenda was set in motion decades earlier and has continued through several presidential administrations. This agenda has been steadily advanced regardless of whether the president was a Republican or a Democrat.

Seemingly unrelated developments in different parts of the world often combine to achieve a common goal. Different strands that appear to operate independently can effectively work toward a singular agenda. This exemplifies what we discussed earlier in this book as piecemeal functionalism—yet another manifestation of evil infiltrations.

As a student of Bible prophecy and someone who has closely followed world events for most of my life, I feel confident in saying we should prepare for unprecedented political, economic, and military crises. I believe these crises will feed off one another, significantly impacting policy shifts, priorities, and freedoms. Such shifts will likely contribute to a full collapse of monetary systems worldwide. Again, this is my opinion; I do not claim to be a prophet, but I share these thoughts based on my understanding of our current times.

We must recognize both the power and the individual who has been staged to fill the powerful vacuum by introducing a leader capable of leading a global government.

I may be mistaken, but I believe the Antichrist is alive today, likely somewhere in Europe or possibly the Middle East. Some contend he is being groomed by Satan himself to assume his global leadership role at this very moment. A pathway is being developed for his rise to power by powerful globalist billionaires who are funding the most liberal individuals they can find to support shadow governments and deep-state actors around the world. This satanic cabal aims to destroy America on every front—be it ethics, religion, economics, or otherwise. Their evil infiltration is quite evident.

These satanically influenced individuals are embedded in every sector of government, media, and entertainment. They have powerful representation across all these domains. The unchecked increases in our federal budget deficit and national debt, coupled with the Federal Reserve's expanding money supply, could soon push America to the brink of collapse.

The following paragraph was written by me in 2019.

As I write this book, most financial indicators are strong—July 2019. (DONALD TRUMP WAS PRESIDENT.) The stock market is at an all-time high, unemployment is at an all-time low, and economically speaking, conditions seem optimal. However, the concerning reality is that we continue to throw money at every aspect of life, causing debt to grow faster than we can manage, with little regard or concern from the public. We are currently $23 trillion in debt and rising. If leftist policies like the "Green New Deal" are implemented, our debt could skyrocket to over $100 trillion. In my opinion, these scenarios could ultimately lead to an economic collapse and the possible acceptance of a World Currency.

Back to 2024…

As of August 2024, our national debt stands at $35 trillion. Regardless of how severe the federal debt becomes, I believe America will recover. For now, it's essential to stay informed and plan for your family's future. First and foremost, invite Christ into your life and follow God's laws; doing so will guide you through challenges.

I want to address a few points about America and Israel. America was the first country to recognize Israel as a nation. Just 11 minutes after David Ben-Gurion raised the Israeli flag on May 14, 1948, President Harry Truman recognized Israel's sovereignty, and America has supported Israel ever since.

Many past presidents claimed they would recognize Jerusalem as Israel's capital but hesitated due to potential diplomatic tensions. However, on December 6, 2017, President Donald Trump formally recognized Jerusalem as the capital of Israel and initiated plans to relocate the U.S. Embassy from Tel Aviv to Jerusalem.

In 2019, President Trump declared the Golan Heights to be Israeli territory and attempted to negotiate with Hamas regarding the Gaza Strip. Unfortunately, this did not come to fruition, and Trump was not re-elected. However, I believe he would have succeeded had he been given a second term. Many people suspect that the 2020 election was manipulated by elites seeking to continue their agenda of establishing a global system from within the White

House. The current administration (Biden) is failing to support Israel adequately. If Kamala Harris is elected in 2024, we can expect the situation to deteriorate further, as she is aligned with the Deep State and many in Congress who support Hamas. By the time you read this, the 2024 election results will have been decided. May God help us if Harris is elected. I apologize for the political tone, but we are at a crossroads—not just between candidates, but between good and evil. The Bible clearly states that those who bless Israel will be blessed, while those who curse Israel will be cursed.

The United States faces a choice: we can follow God's guidance by supporting Israel and receive blessings, or we can align with the world in condemning Israel and incur curses. Historically, most of our presidents have supported Israel. Former President Barack Obama raised concerns with his lack of support for Israel and attempted to oust Prime Minister Benjamin Netanyahu during the Israeli elections. Thankfully, Netanyahu survived and remains in office as of August 2024.

I believe President Trump's decision to withdraw the U.S. from several global treaties and pursue individual agreements with other countries sets us apart from other globalist nations. I want to highlight a couple of points regarding possible future events in the United States. In the Book of Daniel, Chapter 7, Daniel shares a vision of four great beasts. The first beast resembles a lion with eagle's wings, which some interpret as Great Britain and the United States. He also sees a bear (often interpreted as Russia) and a leopard (believed to represent Germany). I'm not claiming these interpretations are definitive, but they are intriguing to consider. Notably, in the Book of Revelation, Chapter 13, the eagle is absent. Could it be that God has prepared the eagle (the United States) to protect Israel during the Tribulation? This is purely speculative; we know God can protect Israel in His own way. Nevertheless, it's a fascinating scenario given that our country has historically supported Israel more than any other nation. Thus, I believe God will bless us.

Conversely, our nation seems to have lost its moral compass and has spiraled downward spiritually. We have permitted sin to infiltrate our laws. Since Roe v. Wade was enacted, millions of babies have been aborted, even up to the point of birth. Drug use is becoming normalized, and our immigration system is broken, with little concern from the populace. The Bible warns that lawlessness will abound in the last days. Some U.S. cities have declared themselves sanctuary cities, defying federal laws. This is yet another example of evil infiltration within our government.

As the time approaches for the Antichrist to emerge, globalists advocating for a world government realize that a system will be necessary to control the masses. Today, we are regulated, restricted, socially engineered, and constantly monitored. Our lives are increasingly directed in ways that favor the government but disadvantage individuals. We are watched and recorded at all times, making it challenging to keep our thoughts private.

Since 2001, under the guise of combating terrorism, our rights have gradually eroded. The so-called elites refer to this as "piecemeal functionalism"—the incremental loss of rights that goes unnoticed because it occurs in small portions rather than a single significant event. This process is part of what we discussed earlier in this book as "management by crisis."

With the advent of email, every message sent or received can be stored and accessed, exposing our private communications. Cell phones allow the government to listen in on conversations and track our exact locations. If authorities wish to find you, they can. This represents an insidious invasion of our privacy rights. Authorities no longer need to plant bugs or listening devices; we have inadvertently equipped our homes with devices capable of monitoring us, often with both audio and video capabilities. I believe future technologies will profoundly impact our society, enabling devices to reveal our whereabouts and actions at all times. We are now entering an era of biometrics, where the use of biometric data is becoming commonplace in our daily lives. Cyber attacks are an ongoing reality in finance, prompting banks to explore super-secure biometric recognition technology to enhance account safety.

Biometric authentication is expected to become mainstream within the next five years. This technology does not merely capture images of faces, fingerprints, or voices but measures hundreds of distinct characteristics and processes them through a proprietary algorithm to create a unique template, as noted in an article by Pat Esswein in "Mobile Press News".

Another article by Lauren Zumbach in the "Chicago Tribune" highlights that biometric payment methods are easier to use than remembering passwords and offer enhanced security since biometric data are difficult to steal. As we embrace sophisticated technology, we find ourselves increasingly accepting facial recognition and fingerprint authentication. The Bible speaks of a time when the Antichrist will demand that we accept a mark on our foreheads or hands. Are we unknowingly accepting these technologies, paving the way for the Antichrist's demands? While I am not asserting this is the specific method the Antichrist will use, it could be a similar process that people readily accept. According to the Bible, refusal to comply will result in the inability to buy or sell, leading to great persecution for those who reject the Antichrist. As believers, we will not be here when the Antichrist begins to impose his demands.

Globalism is being aggressively promoted by organizations such as the World Economic Forum, the World Health Organization, the United Nations, and the G20 nations. These entities are working toward a unified world government. The Covid-19 pandemic has highlighted how global crises can unify the world's focus, leading to demands for peace and safety from governments. The ultimate aim of orchestrated global crises appears to be the establishment of a One-World Government.

Klaus Schwab of the World Economic Forum admires the way China manages its population. According to Wikipedia, there are over 700 million cameras monitoring citizens in China. As of 2019, it was estimated that the "Skynet" system had deployed around 200 million surveillance cameras in mainland China—four times the number in the United States. By 2020, the total was projected to reach 626 million. As of August 2023, this number had surpassed 700 million.

As the level of control over a population increases, so does the risk of dictatorship. The executive orders issued enthusiastically by the Biden administration are concerning, demonstrating how globalism is infiltrating once-democratic governments, pushing them toward a more authoritarian model akin to China.

In my observation, I conclude that China and Russia are increasingly adopting a nationalistic stance as a counter to the growing globalist agenda. This raises questions about nationalism in the context of end-time Bible prophecy. If the world is trending toward globalism, what becomes of these two superpowers?

According to Ezekiel 38-39, the Bible foretells that Russia will move south when Israel is supposedly secure in their land. God will set a hook in Russia's jaw, compelling it to invade Israel. Alongside Russia, Islamic nations allied with it will join in this great Gog-Magog war, only to realize that God will annihilate the invading armies.

The devastated forces of Russia and its Islamic allies may create a power vacuum, facilitating the Antichrist's rise. If the Gog-Magog war occurs around the time of the Rapture, the European Union could emerge as the last superpower. When the Antichrist rises from Europe, as many prophecy teachers believe, his peace accord may allow Israel to rebuild the Temple on the Temple Mount.

This would set the stage for the fulfillment of biblical prophecy. As time progresses, we see more pieces falling into place, providing a clearer picture of how these prophetic events will unfold.

WE ARE WITNESSING A RAPID ACCELERATION OF SIGNS

indicating the nearing Rapture and subsequent Tribulation. The knowledge that Jesus is coming soon instills a sense of expectancy among Christians. This urgency compels us to share the Good News with our lost loved ones.

The rise of globalism is undeniable. As Christians, we need not fear the Antichrist, as we know from the signs that Jesus is coming soon. Our Lord will soon call His children to "Come up Here," and we will be with our Savior for eternity.

By the time the Antichrist is revealed, Christians will have been raptured. The Bible states that we are not destined for wrath. As you witness the development of technologies that the Antichrist may utilize, reflect on how close we might be to the Rapture.

While no one knows the exact time of His return, the Bible instructs us in Thessalonians not to be ignorant of these matters. We, as followers of Christ, are children of light, not of darkness. Therefore, I encourage you to consider your standing with the Lord. Those left behind after the Rapture will face dire consequences.

The extraordinary events anticipated in the coming months and years should prompt many to contemplate the future.

Public interest in biblical prophecies concerning the last days is growing. The impending crises present a valuable opportunity to discuss preparation and share our faith in Christ. Being a saved, born-again Christian will be our anchor during these tumultuous times. In 2 Kings 20:1, we are reminded to "set your house in order."

In my view, the agenda of a Satanic cabal aims to take control of the world through individuals wielding influence and power. They seek to recruit followers by infiltrating media, education, and political spheres. Our children receive indoctrination rather than education in universities, largely due to liberal professors shaped by existing systems.

This cabal is deeply committed to controlling the world through darkness, using influencers to sway unsuspecting followers toward their political ideologies. Satan seeks to dominate the globe, causing suffering and persecution for Christ's followers.

As believers, we must protect our minds and those of our family members with God's word daily.

I recognize that some may criticize me as a doomsday prophet, and that's acceptable to me. My hope is that this message awakens awareness of the current landscape and leads readers to accept Christ as Savior, enabling them to escape the coming tribulations. I genuinely believe we are living in the end times. Believers, remain vigilant and prepared, for at an unexpected hour, the Son of Man will come (Matthew 24:44).

FINAL THOUGHTS

FINAL THOUGHTS

My wife, Gwen, and I recently visited my dear friends Joel and Cathy Estis in Nashville, Tennessee. During our trip, we took a ride around the city and its surroundings. We discovered an artist named David Arms and purchased one of his paintings—a beautiful piece featuring colorful birds in their natural habitat. In the center of the painting, he showcased a page of notebook paper written by his young daughter. Her report was a creative writing assignment given by her teacher, who prompted the class with the first sentence. The teacher had written: "I saw a New Heaven and a New Earth," and the child continued it beautifully:

"My eyes saw things I had never seen before, and my ears heard sounds I had never heard. I saw gardens so perfect that nothing was wilted or dead, and every bloom was glorious. I saw colors that did not exist on Earth. Everything was bright. Everyone was finally happy and content. We were never hungry. The homes were draped with sheer white fabric, and the furniture was made of clouds.

I heard hundreds of thousands of angels singing praises to God. I saw Jesus going through the crowd, hugging everyone. God sat on a gold and red throne where we could go hug Him and ask questions. It will be the best day of my life."

1 Corinthians 2:9 states: "Eye has not seen, ear has not heard, neither has it entered into the heart of man what God has prepared for those who love Him." What the child described merely scratches the surface of what awaits us. Revelation 21:4 reassures us: "He will wipe away every tear from their eyes, and death shall be no more, neither shall there be mourning, nor crying, nor pain anymore, for the former things have passed away."

Songwriter Dottie Rambo penned a chorus that beautifully encapsulates this hope: "Tears will never stain the streets of that city, no wreaths of death on my mansion's door. Teardrops aren't welcome beyond the gates of glory, for the heart will never break anymore." Heaven is a place beyond human imagination. We will see, touch, hear, and smell things that surpass anything we've experienced on Earth.

In Revelation 22:7, Jesus declares, "Behold, I come quickly; blessed is he who keeps the sayings of the prophecy of this book." He reiterates in Revelation 22:20, "Surely, I come quickly."

If you have not yet accepted Jesus as your Lord and Savior, I urge you to do so today. You will never regret your decision.

Maranatha!

ABOUT THE AUTHOR

Dalton Walley, originally from Semmes, Alabama, is a graduate of Mary G. Montgomery High School. A lifelong learner, Dalton has pursued knowledge through independent reading, studying, and research. After many years working as a grocery store manager, he transitioned to a career in the insurance industry, where he remained until his retirement.

Dalton's deep interest in Bible prophecy began when he was just nine years old, sparking a lifelong journey of exploring the unfolding of end-times events. Over the decades, he has dedicated himself to studying how these prophecies align with world events, offering keen insights into their relevance in today's world.

Dalton is a devoted family man. His wife, Gwen Walley, is his rock—wise, courageous, and always putting others first. His son, Devin Walley, is known for his hard work and big heart, always willing to help those in need. His daughter, Deanna Cooke, despite living at a distance, remains closely connected and supportive. Dalton's stepson, James Orr, is a gifted teacher and singer, always ready to go above and beyond for others. His stepdaughter, Vicki Goss, is an intelligent and talented teacher, who, like the rest of the family, is always there to lend a helping hand.

Dalton's faith is at the center of his life, and he credits God for giving His only begotten Son, Jesus Christ, as a ransom for his sins. His unwavering faith has shaped both his personal and professional life, inspiring him to share his insights with others.

REFERENCES

1. Donald Stamps, "The Full Life Study Bible", King James Version. Copyright 1992 by Life Publishers International. All rights reserved. Published by Zondervan Publishing House, Grand Rapids, Michigan.
2. A.A. Ledford, "Trial of Alfred Dreyfus", "Pathways to Prophetic Fulfillment". Copyright 1978 Pathway Press, and Wikipedia.
3. Balfour Declaration—The Basics, Wikipedia.
4. Theodor Herzl—Wikipedia.
5. Wikipedia.
6. A.A. Ledford, "Pathways to Prophetic Fulfillment". Copyright 1978 Pathway Press.
7. History of Adolf Hitler—Wikipedia.
8. History of the European Union—Wikipedia, (Thought Co.).
9. CNS News (www.cnsnews.com/bog/walter-ewilliams/global-warming-religion).
10. https://www.youtube.com (9/11/1991).
11. Craig Crawford, "The Prophecies: A Journey to the End of Time". Copyright by Craig Crawford, First Published 1999, Published by Prophecy Press.

www.ingramcontent.com/pod-product-compliance
Lightning Source LLC
LaVergne TN
LVHW051956060526
838201LV00059B/3680